FIRST PAST THE POST®

Verbal Reasoning: Grammar and Spelling

Multiple Choice

Practice Tests

BOOK 2

How to use this book to make the most of 11 plus exam preparation

It is important to remember that for 11 plus exams there is no national syllabus, no pass mark and no retake option! It is therefore vitally important that your child is fully primed in order to perform to the best of their ability to give themselves the best possible chance on the day.

Unlike similar publications, the First Past the Post® series uniquely assesses your child's performance on a question-by-question basis relative to peers helping to identify areas for improvement and further practice.

CEM Verbal Reasoning Tests

CEM Verbal Reasoning Tests consists of short timed tests with a mixture of verbal reasoning questions. Logic, vocabulary and time management skills are assessed with these practice tests.

Never has it been more useful to learn from mistakes!

Students can improve by as much as 15 percent, not only by focused practice but also by targeting any weak areas.

How to manage your child's own practice

To get the most up-to-date information, log on to the Eleven Plus Exams website (www.elevenplusexams.co.uk). Eleven Plus Exams is the largest UK online resource with over 40,000 webpages and a forum administered by a select group of experienced moderators.

About the authors

The Eleven Plus Exams **First Past the Post®** series has been created by a team of experienced tutors and authors from leading British universities including Oxford and Cambridge.

Published by University of Buckingham Press

With special thanks to the children who tested our material at the Eleven Plus Exams centre in Harrow.

Please note the UBP is not associated with CEM or The University of Durham in any way. This book does not include any official questions and it is not endorsed by CEM or The University of Durham.
CEM, Centre for Evaluation and Monitoring, Durham University and *The University of Durham* are all trademarks of The University of Durham.

ISBN: 9781908684790

About Us

ElevenPlusExams is the UK's largest website offering a vast amount of information and advice, a moderated online forum, books, downloadable materials and online services to enhance your child's chances of success in the demanding selective schools entrance exams, namely the 11+ and common entrance exams.

The company also provides specialist 11+ tuition and is a supplier of online services to schools.

ElevenPlusExams is recognised as a trusted and authoritative source of information and advice. It has been quoted in numerous national newspapers (including The Telegraph, The Sunday Observer, The Daily Mail, The Sunday Telegraph), BBC Radio and national television (BBC1 and Channel 4).

Set up in 2004, the website grew from an initial 20 webpages to more than 65,000 today and has been visited by millions of parents.

The website gives parents impartial advice on preparation, techniques, 11+ exams in their area and preparation material based on actual experience. The forum is the largest for 11+ in the UK, and is moderated by over 20 experts including parents, experienced tutors and authors who collectively provide support both before the exams, and for those parents who are also unfortunate enough to have to appeal the decisions.

Visit our website to benefit from the wealth of information and advice and see why we are the market's leading 'one-stop-shop' for all your eleven plus needs.

- ✓ Comprehensive quality content and advice written by 11+ experts

- ✓ 11+ Online Shop supplying a wide range of practice books, e-papers, software and apps

- ✓ UK's largest online 11+ Forum moderated by experts

- ✓ Lots of FREE practice papers to download

- ✓ Professional tuition services optimising state of the art technology

- ✓ Short Revision courses

- ✓ Year long 11+ courses

- ✓ Mock exams tailored to mirror those of the main examining bodies

11 + Essentials CEM Style Practice Tests

Verbal Reasoning: Cloze Tests
Book 1
9781908684288

Verbal Reasoning: Cloze Tests
Book 2

Verbal Reasoning: Grammar and
Spelling Multiple Choice Books 1 & 2
9781908684646 | 9781908684790

Verbal Reasoning: Vocabulary
Multiple Choice Books 1 & 2
9781908684639 | 9781908684783

Numerical Reasoning: Multi-part
Books 1 & 2
9781908684301 | 9781908684363

Numerical Reasoning: Multi-part
(Multiple Choice) Books 1 & 2
9781908684769 | 9781908684776
NEW for 2016

Numerical Reasoning: Quick-fire
Books 1 & 2
9781908684431 | 9781908684448

Numerical Reasoning: Quick-fire
(Multiple Choice) Books 1 & 2
9781908684653 | 9781908684752
NEW for 2016

English: Comprehensions
Book 1
9781908684295

English: Comprehensions
Book 2
9781908684486

3D Non-Verbal Reasoning
Book 1
9781908684318

3D Non-Verbal Reasoning
Book 2
9781908684479

Mental Arithmetic
Book 1
9781908684462

Numerical Reasoning:
Worded Problems
Book 1
9781908684806
NEW for 2016

Maths Dictionary
9781908684493

NEW for 2016

11 + Practice Paper Packs

Non-Verbal Reasoning
Practice Papers
9781908684134

English
Practice Papers
9781908684103

Verbal Reasoning
Practice Papers
9781908684127

Mathematics
Practice Papers
9781908684110

Contents

Each practice test has a timer that indicates the recommended time within which you should complete the test.

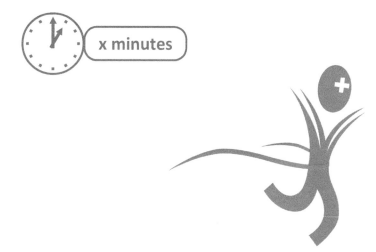

BLANK PAGE

Test 1

Perfect the Grammar

 10 minutes

Marking Grid: Perfect the Grammar												
Question	1	2	3	4	5	6	7	8	9	10	11	Total
✓ ✗												
	12	13	14	15	16	17	18	19	20	21	22	
✓ ✗												/22

For each question, circle the letter of the only option with wholly correct grammar. Choose one out of the four options.

Example	A	It's sad that the dog has a cut on its leg.
	B	Its sad that the dog has a cut on it's leg.
	C	Its sad that the dog has a cut on its leg.
	D	It's sad that the dog has a cut on its' leg.

(Option B is circled)

Question	Option	Sentence
1	A	Niki's knee was bleeding; she needed a plaster.
	B	Niki's knee was bleeding, she needed a plaster
	C	Niki's knee was bleeding: she needed a plaster.
	D	Niki's knee was bleeding she needed a plaster.
2	A	The brothers's toys were scattered all over the room.
	B	The brothers' toys was scattered all over the room
	C	The brothers' toys were scattered all over the room.
	D	The brothers toys were scattered all over the room.
3	A	There going to move into their new house.
	B	They're going to move into their new house.
	C	They're going to move into there new house.
	D	Their going to move into they're new house.
4	A	How many books do you have?
	B	How much books do you have?
	C	How many book do you have?
	D	How much book does you have?
5	A	I think you should apologise to him, Sally.
	B	I think, you should apologise to him Sally.
	C	Sally, you should apologise to him I think.
	D	I think you should apologise to him Sally.

Question	Option	Sentence
6	A	I did not know who's jacket I had mistakenly taken.
	B	I didnt know whose jacket I had mistakenly taken
	C	I didn't know who's jacket I had mistakenly taken.
	D	I did not know whose jacket I had mistakenly taken.
7	A	She was the girl whom helped me yesterday.
	B	She was the girl which helped me yesterday.
	C	She was the girl who helped me yesterday.
	D	She was the girl what helped me yesterday.
8	A	He may have been the man you seen last night.
	B	He may have been the man you saw last night.
	C	He may have been the man you see last night.
	D	He may has been the man you saw last night.
9	A	The childrens became hyper after they ate the sweets.
	B	The children become hyper after they eaten the sweets.
	C	The children became hyper after they eaten the sweets.
	D	The children became hyper after they ate the sweets.
10	A	If it's sunny tomorrow: we will go to the beach.
	B	If its sunny tomorrow, we will go to the beach.
	C	If it's sunny tomorrow, we will go to the beach.
	D	If its sunny tomorrow...we will go to the beach.
11	A	Cassie risen her hand because she knew the answer.
	B	Cassie arose her hand because she knew the answer.
	C	Cassie raised her hand because she knew the answer.
	D	Cassie rised her hand because she knew the answer.

Question	Option	Sentence
12	A	I can't believe it, can you?
	B	I can't believe it can you?
	C	I can't believe it; can you?
	D	I can't believe it: can you?
13	A	He make sure that he done his homework before he left for the party.
	B	He make sure that he did his homework before he left for the party.
	C	He made sure that he done his homework before he left for the party.
	D	He made sure that he did his homework before he left for the party.
14	A	He wasn't sure whether or not it was going to rain.
	B	He wasn't sure either or not it was going to rain.
	C	He wasn't sure neither or not it was going to rain.
	D	He wasn't sure weather or not it was going to rain.
15	A	Your going to have the time of your life!
	B	You're going to have the time of your life!
	C	Your going to have the time of you're life!
	D	You're going to have the time of you're life!
16	A	I need to be up early tomorrow, I should set an alarm.
	B	I need to be up early tomorrow; I should set an alarm.
	C	I need to be up early tomorrow I should set an alarm.
	D	I need to be up early tomorrow... I should set an alarm.
17	A	Neither Karen or Julia wanted to order pizza tonight.
	B	Either Katie nor Julia wanted to order pizza tonight.
	C	Neither Karen nor Julia wanted to order pizza tonight.
	D	Either Karen and Julia wanted to order pizza tonight.

Question	Option	Sentence
18	A	"My kitten," said Shanill, "is called Marbles."
	B	"My kitten" said Shanill "is called Marbles"
	C	"My kitten." said Shanill, "is called Marbles."
	D	"My kitten" said Shanill, "is called Marbles"
19	A	Out of all the flavours I liked toffee the most.
	B	Out of all the flavour I liked toffee the most.
	C	Out of all the flavours, I likes toffee the more.
	D	Out of all the flavours, I liked toffee mostest.
20	A	If you'd arrived on time we wouldnt have a problem.
	B	If you'd arrived on time, we wouldn't have a problem.
	C	If you've arrived on time, we wouldn't have a problem.
	D	If you've arrived on time, we wouldn't had a problem.
21	A	I asked Kate to join Samuel and me later this afternoon.
	B	I asked Kate to join me and Samuel later this afternoon.
	C	I asked Kate to join Samuel and I later this afternoon.
	D	I asked Kate to join I and Samuel later this afternoon.
22	A	Quietly, he sneaked in through the back door.
	B	Quietly he, sneaked in through the back door.
	C	Quietly he sneaked, in through the back door.
	D	Quietly he sneaked in through, the back door.

BLANK PAGE

Test 2

Sentence Completion

 6 minutes

Marking Grid: Sentence Completion													
Question	1	2	3	4	5	6	7	8	9	10	11	12	Total
✓ ✗													
	13	14	15	16	17	18	19	20	21	22	23		
✓ ✗													/23

For each question, circle the letter next to the word that best completes the sentence. Choose one out of the five options.

Example		The dog ___ its dinner.
	A	drank
	B	threw
	C	washed
	D	walked
	(E)	ate

Question	Option	Sentence
1		The magician removed his cape with a _____.
	A	brandish
	B	clench
	C	flourish
	D	surprise
	E	unleash
2		Having lived together for two years, the soldiers felt a sense of _____.
	A	isolation
	B	camaraderie
	C	adventure
	D	crime
	E	friends
3		The boy had a nervous _____, so disliked meeting new people.
	A	deception
	B	declension
	C	disruption
	D	disposition
	E	deflection

Question	Option	Sentence
4		The blazing heat ___ all around.
	A	lived
	B	submerged
	C	imbibed
	D	insulated
	E	radiated
5		The Prime Minister arrived with a large ___ of economists and advisers.
	A	retina
	B	confidence
	C	retinue
	D	conspiracy
	E	rebuke
6		The playwright ___ his work with a 'joie de vivre'.
	A	imbued
	B	merged
	C	annulled
	D	canvassed
	E	transmitted
7		After her prophecies had been fulfilled, there was no doubt the psychic was ___.
	A	aristocratic
	B	supreme
	C	mythic
	D	incorrect
	E	clairvoyant

Question	Option	Sentence
8		"Check we're not being watched," she said, while looking around ___.
	A	furtively
	B	confidently
	C	zealously
	D	anonymously
	E	capriciously
9		The large response to the news story was ___.
	A	mediocre
	B	responsive
	C	unrealistic
	D	fatal
	E	unprecedented
10		They needed to ___ the camp before the enemy arrived.
	A	fortify
	B	revenge
	C	mend
	D	canvass
	E	close
11		The jury had decided: he should be ___.
	A	trusted
	B	quit
	C	guilty
	D	acquitted
	E	debated

Question	Option	Sentence
12		Sherlock Holmes announced that they must ___ the criminal's plans at all costs.
	A	acknowledge
	B	doubt
	C	foil
	D	reimburse
	E	adjust

reimburse = pay back/ repay

13		Once he was assured that the risks were ___, David let the children climb the cliffs.
	A	negligible
	B	significant
	C	adequate
	D	fortunate
	E	robust

negligible = tiny/trace/ most insignificant

14		The politician's argument was ___ and did not fool the opposition.
	A	thorough
	B	misunderstood
	C	bleak
	D	weak
	E	macabre

speaker

15		The orator spoke with great clarity, ___ every syllable.
	A	spelling
	B	clarifying
	C	whispering
	D	shouting
	E	enunciating

enunciating = pronouncing

Question	Option	Sentence

16 While his daughter was diligent and hard-working, his son had succumbed to a

- A religious
- B profligate
- C affluent
- D impractical
- E insane

17 Unfortunately, their scheme lacked ___.

- A cohesion
- B contention
- C comprehension
- D convention
- E competition

18 The jobs she had held over her lifetime indicated a clear career ___.

- A recluse
- B trajectory
- C genius
- D conclusion
- E notion

19 She ___ the faulty thermometer.

- A tuned
- B recalibrated
- C synthesised
- D shook
- E threw

Question	Option	Sentence
20		Since the divorce, there had been a ___ between her parents.
	A	finesse
	B	jeopardy
	C	tear
	D	chasm
	E	path
21		Simon typed in the password ___.
	A	digit
	B	details
	C	letter
	D	lock
	E	combination
22		To give the man some privacy, the nurse installed ___ around his bed.
	A	sheets
	B	walls
	C	windows
	D	partitions
	E	barriers
23		The council reminded them that those who did not pay their rent would be forcibly
	A	evicted
	B	exonerated
	C	evinced
	D	expelled
	E	expunged

evict = kick out
expell = banish/sent away

BLANK PAGE

Test 3

Change A Letter

 15 minutes

Marking Grid: Change A Letter																				
Question	1	2	3	4	5	6	7	8	9	10	11	12	13	14	15	16	17	18	19	20	Total
✓ ✗																					
	21	22	23	24	25	26	27	28	29	30	31	32	33	34	35	36	37	38	39	40	
✓ ✗																					/40

Test 3 - Change A Letter

15 minutes

For each question, change one letter to create a new word that match the definition given. Write the new word in the space provided.

Example	C R A <u>N</u> E	Large storage box	C R A <u>T</u> E

Question	Word	Definition	Answer
1	TONE	a sizeable book	_____
2	ENGAGE	to anger somebody or something	_____
3	BELLOW	an archaic term for a man	_____
4	FOWL	to emit a loud and extended sound of anguish	_____
5	PEEL	loud ringing sound	_____
6	BROUGHT	a description of a metal that has been worked	_____
7	MURAL	an ethical principle	_____
8	GALLOP	unit of measurement for liquids	_____
9	HOARSE	tough and bristly	_____
10	FLOAT	to break or disregard a rule	_____
11	ALL	to trouble or afflict someone	_____
12	BURY	intense anger	_____
13	SLEDGE	thick, semi-liquid waste	_____
14	CONVENT	to agree to something	_____
15	AROSE	plain speech, as opposed to verse	_____
16	BASE	without difficulty	_____
17	THIEF	the leader of a group of people, especially in a tribe	_____
18	GRAIL	the seed for agricultural crops and cereals	_____
19	COMPUTE	the typical daily journey to work	_____
20	PROJECT	to deliver from harm or conserve	_____

Question	Word	Definition	Answer
21	LEMON	a spirit from the underworld	_____
22	ELATE	a select group of people	_____
23	COME	an object used for de-tangling hair	_____
24	FAUN	an immature deer	_____
25	FLESH	a short burst of light	_____
26	BEAKY	small, keen and glinting	_____
27	REED	to draw in, either literally or figuratively	_____
28	OBJECT	intensely unpleasant and degrading	_____
29	THYME	a description of words whose endings sound similar	_____
30	WAIL	a homeless child	_____
31	COMPETE	the presenter in an entertainment arena	_____
32	DIVERGE	representing a variety	_____
33	IDIOT	a peculiar but conventional turn of phrase	_____
34	HOPE	to deal with or manage a situation	_____
35	ALTER	a table used as the focus of religious ceremonies	_____
36	UNIFY	the state of being united as a whole	_____
37	DISPENSE	to scatter or spread over a wide area	_____
38	BRAIN	a plait	_____
39	ATTACK	to connect to something	_____
40	SLATE	a flattish piece of crockery	_____

BLANK PAGE

Test 4

Left Over Word

 22 minutes

Marking Grid: Left Over Word																			
Question	1	2	3	4	5	6	7	8	9	10	11	12	13	14	15	16	17	18	19	Total
✓ ✗																				
	20	21	22	23	24	25	26	27	28	29	30	31	32	33	34	35	36	37	38	
✓ ✗																				/38

Test 4 - Left Over Word

20 minutes

For each question, rearrange the words in the correct order and write a sentence. Underline the extra, unnecessary word.

Example
homework done Joe his hadn't <u>anymore</u>
Joe hadn't done his homework .

1 homework week is this the teacher easy

2 us sister won't to Lisa listen

3 noisy me particularly are the today builders

4 hopefully in summer Spain to am I holiday going my at

5 cold snow dress so can it in winter warmly

6 be and have famous lots poor day money one of will I

7 government civil mother for works as a my servant at the

8 once I forgotten what came for here in have I

9 choice you will in do think election for the vote who whom

10 my delicious of cream favourite ice this flavour is

11   to would Australia like to am I because see koalas I going already

12   what young desist chattering not their girls the would

13   paints prepared brushes her artist the canvass and

14   for a courageous reputation gained great she war being had

15   am ice so I'm bad rink at liability hurt because the on skating a I

16   role probably Juliet Shakespeare's tragedy most and famous Romeo is

17   life lining believe cloud some a has every people silver

18   Michael's weapons France campaign very was in successful

19   morning I every up alarm rooster's by the crowing wake

20   very please manners important are

21   actors film acclaimed and was director for the critically knighted was the

22   drunk brake it's to while irresponsible very drive

23   ingenious and professor's won the was well deserved invention

24   in sentencing or trial the either acquittal jury ends

25   a word capital begin always a sentence with letter should one

26   travel the my secret world England desire to is around

27   with tea spoon I talk most drink milk to their people

28   learning maths a for prerequisite engineering is understanding

29   never ran sadly my father knew I

30   of incomprehensible to number her due the story was mistakes write

31   the quickly homework on comments your read

32   ambition else tell a has don't anybody that true they everyone secret

33   bright music the many at were lights there disco

34   to the give returned I library overdue my book

35   she have did agree treatment with doctor's the not

36   the choir's heard vicar the when singing he grinned discordant winced

37   last she exhausted she the race was when finished

38   talk silently they listen

FIRST PAST THE POST®

Test 5

Shuffled Sentences

20 minutes

Marking Grid: Shuffled Sentences																			
Question	1	2	3	4	5	6	7	8	9	10	11	12	13	14	15	16	17	18	Total
✓ ✗																			
	19	20	21	22	23	24	25	26	27	28	29	30	31	32	33	34	35	36	
✓ ✗																			/36

For each question, rearrange the words in the correct order to form a sentence.

15 minutes

Example

around Rubik's million the Cubes have been over 350 sold world

Over 350 million Rubik's Cubes have been sold around the world.

---

1   hard successful must you be work to

2   respected all him knew who by was he and loved

3   home eleven and left my aged family I

4   milk ran he the buy to some to shops

5   bankers mistrust people many politicians and

6   window before bed to go remember the to shut you

7   been thought before he never Kevin wrong had that

8   watching homework must before your film finish you the

9   belongings you take with all your please

10   morning for go not could this I walk a

11 important crossing both the it is look road before to ways

12 talent work easily outstrip can hard

13 goods China's electrical export is largest

14 talk your mouth full don't please with

15 already sister I may but be than younger my taller am I

16 Victoria children Queen had nine

17 lead school this am I the playing year play in role the

18 Calais book journey my I on lost the to

19 cracked lightning across and sky the thunder flashed

20 sung baby sleep downstairs for to dinner having the went she

21 envious Jim's he basketballl was stole Songyo because

22 accident nobody unfortunate hurt was the in

23 woman staggered old fell the unconscious and

24   it a alight set pyre build and castaway they suggested the

25   on rocks most children of clambering were the around the

26   boat capsize wind too to sail if you the will the close

27   estuary had she fallen in to the drowned and

28   inexperienced dangerous doctor such was it a with an operation

29   mission abort decided to they the

30   concert to had he entry refused been the

31   well warning fallen had deaf intentioned ears their on

32   ahead the counsellor busy guidance week had a

33   asleep fell armchair he and collapsed into an

34   recommendation of grateful your for am I letter

35   undaunted the scale mountain was she the by of

36   picturesque very admit had to the he village was

Test 6

Spelling Error

 10 minutes

Marking Grid: Spelling Error																		
Question	1	2	3	4	5	6	7	8	9	10	11	12	13	14	15	16	17	18	Total
✓ ✗																			
	19	20	21	22	23	24	25	26	27	28	29	30	31	32	33	34	35	36	
✓ ✗																			/36

Test 6 - Spelling Error

For each question, circle the letter above the word that is spelt incorrectly. Choose one out of the five options.

10 minutes

Example	A	B	C	D	E
	drift	drink	drive	dred	drool

Question

	A	B	C	D	E
1	lithe	litter	licentious	liege	litrally
2	herald	heritige	heroine	heresy	herein
3	flotsam	flute	flotilla	fluorecsent	fluctuate
4	kerb	kindergarden	kindle	kerchief	knead
5	weeve	whether	winsome	weather	whet
6	daunting	debonair	darstardly	debauch	damask
7	ruminate	rumour	ruffle	russet	rustick
8	kerosene	kernel	kidney	kerfufle	keg
9	erupt	eratic	erase	erode	error
10	continum	convoluted	contravene	convoy	contrary

Test 6 - Spelling Error

....continued

Question

	A	B	C	D	E
11	impede	implicit	impitus	impugn	impel
12	snoop	snufle	social	solemn	sobriquet
13	gratify	grotto	grase	gravel	grub
14	adoor	adjoin	adorn	admire	adage
15	boon	boot	bool	boor	book
16	queer	quartz	quay	quell	quary
17	trek	tred	trait	tract	trial
18	literal	litre	limpid	litrate	limpet
19	jokey	jaunty	joviel	journal	joint
20	vagery	valve	vacant	veal	venal
21	yowl	yodel	yeoman	yacht	yolke
22	rebuff	receept	referee	refer	recite
23	plunge	poise	pluc	plague	pivot

Test 6 - Spelling Error

....continued

Question

	A	B	C	D	E
24	modulate	majesty	mallard	mitagate	moist
25	curate	coward	clutch	crucial	corage
26	dismis	dispel	doe	distil	dodge
27	evade	engrose	eschew	exact	equity
28	usher	urge	unweldy	upend	utmost
29	zoology	zeal	zone	zodiak	zenith
30	trespass	trophy	truculent	trifle	tradgedy
31	coloquial	course	column	cauldron	coarse
32	lavae	lackluster	lampoon	language	lagoon
33	simper	silhouette	stratigies	sombre	scheme
34	resources	responsible	radical	repitition	repertoire
35	gorgeous	ghaustly	gremlin	gramophone	goblin
36	inconvenence	inspire	introvert	inviting	incomplete

Test 7

Partial Words

 18 minutes

Marking Grid: Partial Words																			
Question	1	2	3	4	5	6	7	8	9	10	11	12	13	14	15	16	17	18	Total
✓ ✗																			
	19	20	21	22	23	24	25	26	27	28	29	30	31	32	33	34	35	36	
✓ ✗																			/36

For each question, fill in the missing letters to complete the word so that it matches the definition given.

Example
A B U N DANCE   Copious amounts

1   H U ☐ IL ☐ ATE   to embarrass or ridicule

2   S ☐ LHO ☐ ET ☐ EA   profile in shadow

3   E ☐ IL ☐ G ☐ E   a final conclusion or an author's comment at the end of a book

4   AC ☐ ☐ MP ☐ NY   to join and go alongside

5   M ☐ NOL ☐ ☐ UE   a speech made by a single character to an audience

6   I ☐ SE ☐ ☐ RE   lacking in confidence and security

7   CO ☐ ME ☐ D   to praise or recommend

8   EN ☐ O ☐ R ☐ GE   to offer support and confidence

9   C O ☐ ☐ CID ☐ NCE   having no causal connection

10   LU ☐ AT ☐ C   someone who is clinically insane

11 EM☐ATH☐ZE   feeling understanding and pity for another's situation

12 SU☐PL☐S   more than enough

13 PR☐FO☐ND   deep and meaningful

14 RE☐☐L   pertaining to a monarch

15 JE☐PA☐DI☐E   to put in danger

16 PAC☐FI☐T   a person who disbelieves in war

17 FA☐☐INAT☐NG   very interesting

18 CO☐AR☐LY   lacking in courage

19 FO☐TU☐☐TE   lucky

20 FAL☐I☐LE   capable of being wrong

21 GLI☐M☐R   to glint and shine

22 DI☐SO☐VE   to gradually become part of a liquid

23 E☐R☐NT   straying from the accepted course

24   P☐NC☐URE   to cause a hole and deflate

25   Q☐EN☐H   to satisfy thirst

26   CE☐ETE☐Y   burial ground

27   H☐SP☐TA☐ITY   friendly reception of guests

28   RO☐A☐CE   sentimental or idealised love

29   P☐RSE☐ER☐   to continue despite difficulties

30   AR☐IFIC☐A☐   manufactured or false

31   C☐HER☐NT   logical or clear

32   SU☐C☐M☐   to submit to pressure or difficulty

33   PI☐NA☐LE   the highest point or greatest triumph

34   TRA☐ES☐Y   an outrage

35   ME☐A☐CH☐LY   despondent and morose

36   A☐DI☐☐CE   spectators or listeners

Test 8

Synonyms and Antonyms

 25 minutes

Marking Grid: Synonyms and Antonyms																		
Question	1	2	3	4	5	6	7	8	9	10	11	12	13	14	15	16	17	18	Total
✓ ✗																		
	19	20	21	22	23	24	25	26	27	28	29	30	31	32	33	34	35	36	
✓ ✗																			/36

For each question, fill in the missing letters to complete the words so that they form synonyms and antonyms of the given word.

Example	COY	S□Y	B□LD

Question	Word	Synonym	Antonym
1	knowledgeable	ED□C□T□D	I□NO□ANT
2	bravery	C□UR□GE	CO□AR□ICE
3	welcoming	H□SP□T□BLE	AU□T□RE
4	forthcoming	CO□M□NIC□TI□E	R□SE□VED
5	congested	BL□C□ED	E□PT□
6	tedious	M□N□T□NOUS	FA□CI□AT□NG
7	fabrication	FA□SE□OOD	R□AL□TY
8	forgetful	DI□OR□ANI□ED	EF□IC□ENT
9	illustration	E□PLA□A□ION	CO□PL□C□TION
10	grandiose	PR□T□NT□OUS	HU□BL□
11	particular	PE□UL□AR	ORDI□AR□

Question	Word	Synonym	Antonym
12	confrontational	PU☐NA☐IO☐S	SYM☐ATH☐T☐C
13	impinge	EN☐ROAC☐	AV☐☐D
14	necessary	ES☐EN☐IAL	AUX☐LI☐RY
15	destiny	F☐☐E	CO☐NC☐DE☐CE
16	grotesque	HID☐O☐S	CH☐RM☐NG
17	forgery	IM☐T☐T☐ON	OR☐G☐NAL
18	embarrass	S☐AM☐	DE☐IG☐T
19	despicable	LO☐THS☐ME	H☐N☐UR☐BLE
20	transient	FL☐ET☐NG	E☐D☐RING
21	obstinate	ST☐B☐OR☐	YI☐LD☐NG
22	sallow	PA☐LI☐	GL☐WI☐G
23	flummox	C☐NF☐SE	CL☐RI☐Y

Test 8 - Synonyms and Antonyms

....continued

Question	Word	Synonym	Antonym
24	spiteful	HU☐TF☐L	CO☐SI☐ER☐TE
25	trepidation	CA☐TI☐US☐ESS	AS☐ERT☐VE☐ESS
26	advantage	BE☐E☐IT	MI☐FO☐TUNE
27	insidious	DU☐LIC☐TO☐S	SI☐CER☐
28	outcast	ST☐A☐	CI☐IZ☐N
29	flamboyant	PR☐T☐NT☐OUS	SU☐D☐ED
30	synchronize	CO☐RDI☐ATE	DI☐OR☐AN☐SE
31	physical	CO☐PO☐EAL	SP☐R☐TU☐L
32	gratitude	REC☐GN☐TION	DIS☐OU☐TESY
33	awkward	U☐GA☐NLY	GR☐CE☐UL
34	relaxed	IN☐OR☐AL	PE☐ANT☐C
35	devour	GO☐G☐	EJ☐C☐
36	fluctuate	W☐VE☐	R☐MA☐N

FIRST PAST THE POST®

Test 9

Sets of Synonyms

 15 minutes

Marking Grid: Sets of Synonyms																
Question	1	2	3	4	5	6	7	8	9	10	11	12	13	14	15	Total
✓ or ✗																
	16	17	18	19	20	21	22	23	24	25	26	27	28	29	30	
✓ or ✗																/30

Test 9 - Sets of Synonyms

For each question, circle the letter above the set of words that are most similar in meaning to the given word. Choose one out of the four options.

15 minutes

Example	brusquely	A	B	C	D
		quietly	abruptly	soothingly	placidly
		softly	violently	tenderly	peacefully
		lightly	roughly	kindly	calmly
		smoothly	harshly	quietly	coolly

Question	Word		Sets of Synonyms		
1	dejected	**A**	**B**	**C**	**D**
		rebuffed	lost	downcast	evicted
		excluded	desperate	despondent	expelled
		rejected	lonely	wretched	ousted
		spurned	solitary	pitiful	removed
2	callous	**A**	**B**	**C**	**D**
		heartless	inviting	cold	uncertain
		unfeeling	pleasant	austere	doubtful
		ruthless	hospitable	frigid	dubious
		brutal	welcoming	severe	cautious
3	benign	**A**	**B**	**C**	**D**
		reckless	kind	aggressive	fascinating
		rash	caring	vigorous	delightful
		thoughtless	gentle	dynamic	captivating
		immature	amiable	forceful	dazzling
4	equivocal	**A**	**B**	**C**	**D**
		clear	practical	ambiguous	confused
		definite	mechanic	obscure	uncontrolled
		certain	efficient	arguable	anarchic
		apparent	functional	debatable	riotous
5	taciturn	**A**	**B**	**C**	**D**
		charming	responsive	resentful	reserved
		polite	chatty	covetous	reticent
		attentive	communicative	envious	distant
		attractive	garrulous	jealous	aloof
6	delusion	**A**	**B**	**C**	**D**
		project	assignment	misconception	enterprise
		plan	preparation	fantasy	business
		design	chore	dream	effort
		idea	commission	illusion	application

Test 9 - Sets of Synonyms

....continued

Question	Word		Sets of Synonyms		
		A	**B**	**C**	**D**
7	consequence	trivial	outcome	mystery	creation
		unimportant	result	secret	inauguration
		minor	repercussion	myth	introduction
		trifling	effect	puzzle	birth
8	organisation	**A**	**B**	**C**	**D**
		refuge	tidy	system	business
		retreat	neat	arrangement	company
		haunt	efficient	grid	society
		den	clean	lattice	club
9	terse	**A**	**B**	**C**	**D**
		succinct	clever	hard	smooth
		brief	witty	tough	even
		concise	smart	sturdy	flat
		abrupt	bright	resistant	level
10	irk	**A**	**B**	**C**	**D**
		wound	irritate	advance	violate
		damage	agitate	venture	defile
		harm	annoy	embark	desecrate
		impair	vex	undertake	abuse
11	flagrant	**A**	**B**	**C**	**D**
		glaring	savage	energetic	vast
		obvious	vicious	lively	broad
		overt	sadistic	vigorous	ample
		blatant	callous	bustling	wide
12	deplete	**A**	**B**	**C**	**D**
		refuse	retreat	reduce	arrest
		veto	exit	exhaust	impeach
		repudiate	retire	consume	apprehend
		retract	withdraw	empty	detain
13	flaw	**A**	**B**	**C**	**D**
		defect	door	bonus	shelter
		failing	window	benefit	protection
		error	wall	advantage	screen
		imperfection	ceiling	reward	cover

Question	Word	Sets of Synonyms			
		A	**B**	**C**	**D**
14	beckon	stir	scare	illustrate	gesture
		blend	frighten	indicate	sign
		mix	shock	demonstrate	signal
		whisk	terrify	show	attract
15	agony	**A**	**B**	**C**	**D**
		infirmity	estrange	suffering	humanity
		fragility	confuse	pain	goodwill
		weakness	separate	torture	compassion
		instability	alienate	anguish	generosity
16	schism	**A**	**B**	**C**	**D**
		rebellion	division	commission	plan
		uprising	breach	appointment	conspiracy
		mutiny	rift	engagement	idea
		revolt	split	task	strategy
17	spite	**A**	**B**	**C**	**D**
		bravery	delightful	impudence	malice
		daring	agreeable	rudeness	venom
		resolution	pleasurable	audacity	animosity
		courage	considerate	temerity	rancour
18	partial	**A**	**B**	**C**	**D**
		biased	complete	worthy	incomplete
		prejudiced	whole	generous	small
		partisan	entire	upright	lacking
		disposed	total	virtuous	imperfect
19	devotee	**A**	**B**	**C**	**D**
		admirer	servant	client	employee
		disciple	attendant	customer	worker
		enthusiast	maid	patron	colleague
		supporter	domestic	purchaser	assistant
20	wither	**A**	**B**	**C**	**D**
		whether	wilt	appear	release
		either	decay	arise	leak
		if	corrode	surface	discharge
		because	rot	emanate	eject

.

Question	Word	Sets of Synonyms			
		A	**B**	**C**	**D**
21	familiar	vague	assurance	recognised	faculty
		unclear	conviction	common	skill
		muted	trust	ordinary	power
		distant	confidence	routine	ability
22	empire	**A**	**B**	**C**	**D**
		history	generator	foe	kingdom
		account	mechanism	rival	territory
		chronicle	motor	opponent	province
		tale	machine	adversary	realm
23	justification	**A**	**B**	**C**	**D**
		explanation	judgement	projection	justice
		rationale	facility	supposition	fairness
		pretext	knowledge	belief	honour
		vindication	skill	forecast	integrity
24	motivate	**A**	**B**	**C**	**D**
		entail	prompt	grieve	charm
		involve	stimulate	lament	fascinate
		require	drive	bemoan	enchant
		demand	inspire	deplore	captivate
25	embroil	**A**	**B**	**C**	**D**
		involve	disregard	appoint	pilfer
		implicate	ignore	recommend	steal
		entangle	overlook	suggest	misappropriate
		ensnare	omit	propose	purloin
26	mundane	**A**	**B**	**C**	**D**
		strange	motto	banal	enigmatic
		bizarre	dictum	ordinary	paranormal
		puzzling	maxim	prosaic	occult
		perplexing	slogan	humdrum	supernatural
27	proportion	**A**	**B**	**C**	**D**
		portion	objective	pledge	conclusion
		share	goal	vow	finale
		part	aim	promise	climax
		percentage	purpose	swear	consummation

.

Question	Word		Sets of Synonyms		
		A	**B**	**C**	**D**
28	muse	idol	bargain	build	ponder
		celebrity	deal	shape	reflect
		star	barter	fashion	contemplate
		personage	haggle	design	consider
29	inevitable	**A**	**B**	**C**	**D**
		unconventional	unavoidable	civic	melodious
		innovative	inexorable	local	lyrical
		unexpected	inescapable	public	dulcet
		radical	assured	municipal	harmonious
30	flamboyant	**A**	**B**	**C**	**D**
		modest	mad	exuberant	mediocre
		humble	crazy	ostentatious	average
		meek	insane	showy	vanilla
		mild	loony	animated	middling

Test 10

Mixed Test

 40 minutes

For each question, circle the letter of the only option with wholly correct grammar. Choose one out of the four options.

Question	Option	Sentence
1	A	The shopping list contained, milk, bread, soup and tomatoes.
	B	The shopping list contained; milk, bread, soup and tomatoes.
	C	The shopping list contained milk, bread, soup, and tomatoes.
	D	The shopping list contained milk, bread, soup and tomatoes.
2	A	"Who's the best shot" asked the Captain?
	B	"Who's the best shot?" asked the Captain?
	C	"Whose the best shot?" asked the Captain.
	D	"Who's the best shot?" asked the Captain.
3	A	I wouldn't have thought its James's problem.
	B	I wouldn't have thought it's James's problem.
	C	I wouldnt have thought its James's problem.
	D	I wouldnt have thought it's James's problem.
4	A	She assured him the criminal would be hanged.
	B	She assured him the criminal will be hanged.
	C	She assured him the criminal would be hung.
	D	She assured him the criminal will be hung.
5	A	She bid farewell to her parents and boarded the train.
	B	She bidded farewell to her parents and boarded the train.
	C	She bade farewell to her parents and boarded the train.
	D	She bidden farewell to her parents and boarded the train.
6	A	I carefully completed my homework; my teacher dislikes its being messy.
	B	I carefully completed my homework, my teacher dislikes its being messy.
	C	I carefully completed my homework - my teacher dislikes its being messy.
	D	I carefully completed my homework... my teacher dislikes its being messy.

Question	Option	Sentence
7	A	Who did you say was your nephew.
	B	Whom did you say was your nephew?
	C	Which did you say was your nephew?
	D	Who did you say was your nephew?
8	A	I always drink less than five cups of coffee a day.
	B	I always drink less than five cup's of coffee a day.
	C	I always drink fewer than five cups of coffee a day.
	D	I always drink fewer than five cup's of coffee a day.
9	A	I don't eat foods that aren't organic.
	B	I don't eat foods that arent organic.
	C	I dont eat foods that arent organic.
	D	I dont eat foods that aren't organic.
10	A	I asked Bhavika whether she could borrow me her ruler.
	B	I asked Bhavika weather she could borrow me her ruler.
	C	I asked Bhavika whether she could lend me her ruler.
	D	I asked Bhavika weather she could lend me her ruler.

Test - 10 Sentence Completion

For each question, circle the letter next to the word that best completes the sentence. Choose one out of the five options.

Question	Option	Sentence
1		Mr Banks had been particularly ___ that day, and kicked Jack out of the class.
	A	delightful
	B	glum
	C	quick-tempered
	D	conspiratorial
	E	anxious
2		To apologise, she presented him with a ___ of chocolates.
	A	sack
	B	bouquet
	C	gesture
	D	wreath
	E	box
3		I wandered ___ around town waiting for my train.
	A	confidently
	B	awfully
	C	defiantly
	D	aimlessly
	E	meekly
4		Guy Fawkes attempted to kill his monarch, which is an act of ___.
	A	treason
	B	evil
	C	revenge
	D	heresy
	E	murder
5		The policemen decided to make a ___ over the racing outcome.
	A	game
	B	idea
	C	competition
	D	gambler
	E	wager
6		They had lost the map, but Zara used her ___ and asked a local for directions.
	A	intellect
	B	inspiration
	C	inhibition
	D	initiative
	E	inhalation

Question	Option	Sentence
7		Unfortunately, Kiran had not been successful, so I offered him my ___.
	A	commiserations
	B	cancellations
	C	confrontations
	D	creations
	E	congratulations
8		"I thought you were the best," said Maia ___.
	A	hysterically
	B	encouragingly
	C	miserably
	D	distrustfully
	E	argumentatively
9		The play's ___was the main character's betrayal.
	A	scene
	B	conclusion
	C	act
	D	climax
	E	character
10		He wanted to be a chef, but soon realised he didn't know the first thing about ___.
	A	trilogy
	B	geometry
	C	cosmology
	D	hockey
	E	gastronomy

Test 10 - Change A Letter

For each question, change one letter to create a new word that matches the definition given. Write the new word in the space provided.

Question	Word	Definition	Answer
1	BLUSTER	to make someone agitated or upset	_____
2	INSURE	to guarantee the occurrence of something	_____
3	DUEL	consisting of two parts	_____
4	BROOCH	to introduce a subject	_____
5	BIRTH	a bed on a train	_____
6	ASSENT	to go up	_____
7	ADJURE	to publicly reject a belief	_____
8	CHAFF	to rub until sore	_____
9	TURBID	swollen	_____
10	REBUT	first entrance into the public sphere or first performance	_____

Test 10 - Left Over Word

For each question, rearrange the words in the correct order to form a sentence, and underline the extra, unnecessary word.

Question **Sentence**

1 should three each I homework hours' students of have night

2 careless again lives costs talk

3 bouncing the off room across frizbee the and ricocheted ceiling the

4 girl weak lamented grade his student the

5 antonyms are indifference and apathy synonyms

6 anticipated grinning was disappointed not she and objections

7 shuffled learn concentration require sentences

8 holiday I'm two Easter have a week we for

9 café waiting children the cake are in a

10 don't sleep them the babysitter I told need I

For each question, rearrange the words in the correct order to form a sentence.

Question   Sentence

1   skillfully anaesthetic the prepared nurse the

2   Dunkirk captured they at been had

3   hungrily brushed teeth my thoroughly breakfast I gobbled my and

4   accepted tragedy moved and they the on

5   questioning his response nonchalant to gave she a

6   afraid I never been dark have the of

7   sins wrath one the of deadly is seven

8   incorrect unfortunately hypothesis is your

9   farm an unconventional office looked and resembled almost the block

10   glitch the system in the meant results scrambled were the

Test 10 - Spelling Error

For each question, circle the letter above the word that is spelt incorrectly. Choose one out of the five options.

Question	A	B	C	D	E
1	traumatised	tranquil	trope	transient	trampaline
2	yeast	yesterday	yoghut	youthful	yield
3	brunette	brooze	buoy	browse	byre
4	presume	precision	precipice	practise	presise
5	forfate	forage	forlorn	foreign	foliage
6	egregious	efface	excentric	ecstacy	echelon
7	through	throttle	thwack	thaught	thwart
8	notorious	nonplussed	naught	notible	nostalgia
9	mousse	mustache	mosquito	muesli	mussel
10	remediation	ridiculous	ricosheted	rationale	restitution

Test 10 - Partial Words

For each question, fill in the missing letters to complete the word so that it matches the definition given.

Question	Word		Definition
	Word		**Definition**
1	C☐PT☐V☐TE		to procure the attention of someone
2	CO☐G☐ST☐D		blocked up
3	TE☐P☐RA☐Y		lasting for a short while
4	CA☐PA☐GN		fighting towards a goal
5	R☐MI☐ISCE		to look back fondly at the past
6	D☐LIN☐UE☐T		A young offender
7	M☐LIG☐☐NT		characterised by evil
8	N☐UR☐TIC		extremely anxious and obsessive
9	F☐T☐OM		to understand and figure out
10	BR☐V☐D☐		a display of typically masculine self-confidence

Test 10 - Synonyms and Antonyms

For each question, fill in the missing letters to complete the words so that they form synonyms and antonyms of the given word.

Question	Word	Synonym	Antonym
1	overt	CON☐PIC☐O☐S	SU☐TL☐
2	patient	TO☐E☐ANT	FR☐STR☐TED
3	presume	SU☐P☐SE	DIS☐EL☐EVE
4	unconcerned	DIS☐NT☐R☐STED	EX☐I☐ED
5	fiasco	CA☐ASTR☐P☐E	TR☐UM☐H
6	priest	V☐CA☐	C☐NGR☐GAT☐ON
7	tolerate	AB☐D☐	DI☐AL☐OW
8	slander	GO☐S☐P	P☐AI☐E
9	anarchy	LA☐LE☐SNE☐S	AU☐HO☐ITY
10	bountiful	PLE☐TI☐UL	M☐AG☐E

Test 10 - Sets of Synonyms

For each question, circle the letter above the set of words that are most similar in meaning to the given word. Choose one out of the four options.

Question	Word	Sets of Synonyms			

Question	Word	A	B	C	D
1	flamboyant	modest humble meek mild	mad crazy insane loony	exuberant ostentatious showy animated	mediocre average vanilla middling
2	tiresome	sleepy tired exhausted drowsy	tedious monotonous dreary dull	fearsome ferocious fierce fiesty	relaxed eased mitigated alleviated
3	festive	festival celebration holiday party	celebratory jubilant merry jovial	assertive confident forceful decisive	presents cards decorations feasts
4	rowdy	raucous unruly disorderly boisterous	crowd congregation aggregation audience	overcast cloudy grey dreary	calm quiet reserved peaceful
5	hysterical	joking teasing taunting mocking	comedy tragedy history musical	straight serious solemn resolute	overemotional delirious frenzied frantic
6	meticulous	slapdash careless hasty heedless	mischievous cheeky naughty roguish	diligent thorough painstaking scrupulous	obedient compliant dutiful subservient
7	pompous	arrogant proud conceited haughty	pious devout religious pure	modest unassuming mild humble	rigorous conscientious accurate exact

Question	Word	Sets of Synonyms			
		A	**B**	**C**	**D**
8	gregarious	menial	gorgeous	friendly	solitary
		lowly	beautiful	social	lonely
		unskilled	stunning	amiable	unaccompanied
		inferior	striking	convivial	reclusive
9	generate	**A**	**B**	**C**	**D**
		electrical	generation	genial	create
		solar	cohort	genuine	produce
		wind	batch	gentrification	conjure
		nuclear	crop	genocide	foster
10	affluent	**A**	**B**	**C**	**D**
		basic	wealthy	merging	afflicted
		simple	prosperous	confluent	troubled
		elementary	rich	combining	burdened
		fundamental	flush	blending	harassed

Answers

For each question, circle the letter of the only option with wholly correct grammar. Choose one out of the four options.

Pages 2-4		
Q	Answer	Explanation
Eg	A	An apostrophe is required for the contraction 'It's'. The possessive pronoun 'its' does not require an apostrophe.
1	A	A semicolon is required to indicate that the two clauses are related.
2	C	An apostrophe is needed after the word 'brothers' to indicate possession of their toys. A full-stop is needed to complete the sentence.
3	B	'They're' is a contraction of the words 'they are'. The possessive pronoun 'their' is required to indicate that the house belongs to them.
4	A	The words 'many' and 'books' are required as they are both the plural forms of the words.
5	A	A comma is required after the word 'him' in order to establish who is being addressed.
6	D	The relative pronoun 'whose' is required as a substitute for the name of the person.
7	C	The relative pronoun 'who' is required as a substitute for the name of the person.
8	B	The correct form of the verb is 'have'. The correct form of the other verb is 'saw'.
9	D	The plural form of the word 'child' is 'children'. The correct form of the verb is 'became'. The correct form of the verb is 'ate'.
10	C	An apostrophe is needed for the contraction 'it's'. A comma is required after the word 'tomorrow' to separate the clauses of the sentence.
11	C	The correct form of the verb is 'raised'.
12	A	A comma is required after the word 'it' to separate the clauses of the sentence.
13	D	The correct form of the verb is 'made'. The correct form of the other verb is 'did'.
14	A	The conjunction 'whether' is required to link the two halves of the sentence.
15	B	'You're' is a contraction of the words 'you are'.
16	B	A semicolon is required to indicate that the two clauses are related.
17	C	The conjunction 'neither' is required to introduce a negative statement. The word 'neither' must be coupled with the word 'nor'.
18	A	A comma is needed after 'kitten' because it is ending a piece of direct speech. A comma is needed after 'Shanill' because it is introducing a piece of direct speech.
19	A	The word 'most' is required as it is the superlative form of much and many. It indicates the greatest in quantity. Whereas 'more' indicates the comparative form of much and many. The correct form of the verb is 'liked'. The plural form of the word 'flavour' is 'flavours'.
20	B	'You'd' is a contraction of the words 'you had'. A comma is required after the word 'time' to separate the clauses of the sentence.
21	B	The word 'me' is the object pronoun.
22	A	A comma is required after 'quietly' to mark off the introductory clause.

Test 2 - Sentence Completion

For each question, circle the letter next to the word that best completes the sentence. Choose one out of the five options.

Pages 9-14			
Q	Answer	Word	Explanation
Eg	E	ate	The dog ate its dinner.
1	C	flourish	The magician removed his cape with a **flourish**.
2	B	camaraderie	Having lived together for two years, the soldiers felt a sense of **camaraderie**.
3	D	disposition	The boy had a nervous **disposition**, so disliked meeting new people.
4	E	radiated	The blazing heat **radiated** all around.
5	C	retinue	The Prime Minister arrived with a large **retinue** of economists and advisers.
6	A	imbued	The playwright **imbued** his work with a 'joie de vivre'.
7	E	clairvoyant	After her prophecies had been fulfilled, there was no doubt the psychic was **clairvoyant**.
8	A	furtively	"Check we're not being watched," she said, while looking around **furtively**.
9	E	unprecedent-ed	The large response to the news story was **unprecedented**.
10	A	fortify	They needed to **fortify** the camp before the enemy arrived.
11	D	acquitted	The jury had decided: he should be **acquitted**.
12	C	foil	Sherlock Holmes announced that they must **foil** the criminal's plans at all costs.
13	A	negligible	Once he was assured that the risks were **negligible**, David let the children climb the cliffs.
14	D	weak	The politician's argument was **weak** and did not fool the opposition.
15	E	enunciating	The orator spoke with great clarity, **enunciating** every syllable.
16	B	profligate	While his daughter was diligent and hard-working, his son had succumbed to a **profligate** lifestyle.
17	A	cohesion	Unfortunately, their scheme lacked **cohesion**.
18	B	trajectory	The jobs she had held over her lifetime indicated a clear career **trajectory**.
19	B	recalibrated	She **recalibrated** the faulty thermometer.
20	D	chasm	Since the divorce, there had been a **chasm** between her parents.
21	E	combination	Simon typed in the password **combination**.
22	D	partitions	To give the man some privacy, the nurse installed **partitions** around his bed.
23	A	evicted	The council reminded them that those who did not pay their rent would be forcibly **evicted**.

For each question, change one letter to create a new word that matches the definition given.
Write the new word in the space provided.

Pages 16-17		
Question	Answer	Explanation
Example	CRATE	Change N to T
1	TOME	Change N to M
2	ENRAGE	Change the first G to R
3	FELLOW	Change B to F
4	HOWL	Change F to H
5	PEAL	Change the second E to A
6	WROUGHT	Change B to W
7	MORAL	Change U to O
8	GALLON	Change P to N
9	COARSE	Change H to C
10	FLOUT	Change A to U
11	AIL	Change the first L to I
12	FURY	Change B to F
13	SLUDGE	Change the first E to U
14	CONSENT	Change V to S
15	PROSE	Change A to P
16	EASE	Change B to E
17	CHIEF	Change T to C
18	GRAIN	Change L to N
19	COMMUTE	Change P to M
20	PROTECT	Change J to T
21	DEMON	Change L to D
22	ELITE	Change A to I
23	COMB	Change E to B
24	FAWN	Change U to W
25	FLASH	Change E to A
26	BEADY	Change K to D
27	REEL	Change D to L
28	ABJECT	Change O to A
29	RHYME	Change T to R
30	WAIF	Change L to F
31	COMPERE	Change T to R
32	DIVERSE	Change G to S
33	IDIOM	Change T to M
34	COPE	Change H to C
35	ALTAR	Change E to A
36	UNITY	Change F to T
37	DISPERSE	Change N to R
38	BRAID	Change N to D
39	ATTACH	Change K to H
40	PLATE	Change S to P

For each question, rearrange the words in the correct order and write a sentence. Underline the extra, unnecessary word.

	Pages 20-22	
Q	Answer	Explanation
Eg	anymore	Joe hadn't done his homework.
1	teacher	The homework this week is easy.
2	sister	Lisa won't listen to us.
3	me	The builders are particularly noisy today.
4	at	Hopefully I am going to Spain in my summer holiday.
5	cold	It can snow in winter so dress warmly.
6	poor	One day I will be famous and have lots of money.
7	at	My mother works as a civil servant for the government.
8	once	I have forgotten what I came in here for.
9	choice	Who do you think will vote for whom in the election?
10	delicious	This is my favourite flavour of ice cream.
11	already	I am going to Australia because I would like to see koalas.
12	what	The young girls would not desist their chattering.
13	canvass	The artist prepared her paints and brushes.
14	war	She had gained a great reputation for being courageous.
15	hurt	I am a liability on the ice rink because I'm so bad at skating.
16	role	Shakespeare's most famous tragedy is probably Romeo and Juliet.
17	life	Some people believe every cloud has a silver lining.
18	weapons	Michael's campaign in France was very successful.
19	alarm	I wake up every morning by the rooster's crowing.
20	please	Manners are very important.
21	actors	The director was knighted and was critically acclaimed for the film.
22	brake	It's very irresponsible to drive while drunk.
23	won	The professor's invention was ingenious and well deserved.
24	jury	The trial either ends in sentencing or acquittal.
25	word	One should always begin a sentence with a capital letter.
26	England	My secret desire is to travel around the world.
27	spoon	Most people I talk to drink their tea with milk.
28	learning	Maths is a prerequisite for understanding engineering.
29	ran	Sadly I never knew my father.
30	write	Her story was incomprehensible due to the number of mistakes.
31	quickly	Read the comments on your homework.
32	true	Everyone has a secret ambition that they don't tell anybody else.
33	music	There were many bright lights at the disco.
34	give	I returned my overdue book to the library.
35	have	She did not agree with the doctor's treatment.
36	grinned	The vicar winced when he heard the choir's discordant singing.
37	last	She was exhausted when she finished the race.
38	talk	They listen silently.

Test 5 - Shuffled Sentences

For each question, rearrange the words in the correct order to form a sentence.

Pages	26
Q	**Answer**
Eg	Over 350 million Rubik's Cubes have been sold around the world.
1	To be successful you must work hard.
2	He was loved and respected by all who knew him.
3	I left my home and family aged eleven.
4	He ran to the shops to buy some milk.
5	Many people mistrust bankers and politicians.
6	Remember to shut the window before you go to bed.
7	Kevin thought that he had never been wrong before.
8	You must finish your homework before watching the film.
9	Please take all your belongings with you.
10	I could not go for a walk this morning.
11	It is important to look both ways before crossing the road.
12	Hard work can easily outstrip talent.
13	China's largest export is electrical goods.
14	Please don't talk with your mouth full.
15	I may be younger but I am already taller than my sister.
16	Queen Victoria had nine children.
17	I am playing the lead role in the school play this year.
18	I lost my book on the journey to Calais.
19	Thunder cracked and lightning flashed across the sky.
20	Having sung the baby to sleep she went downstairs for dinner.
21	Songyo stole Jim's basketball because he was envious.
22	Nobody was hurt in the unfortunate accident.
23	The old woman staggered and fell unconscious.
24	The castaway suggested they build a pyre and set it alight.
25	Most of the children were clambering around on the rocks.
26	The boat will capsize if you sail too close to the wind.
27	She had fallen into the estuary and drowned.
28	It was a dangerous operation with such an inexperienced doctor.
29	They decided to abort the mission.
30	He had been refused entry to the concert.
31	Their well intentioned warning had fallen on deaf ears.
32	The guidance counsellor had a busy week ahead.
33	He collapsed into an armchair and fell asleep.
34	I am grateful for your letter of recommendation.
35	She was undaunted by the scale of the mountain.
36	He had to admit the village was very picturesque.

Test 6 - Spelling Error

For each question, circle the letter above the word that is spelt incorrectly. Choose one out of the five options.

Pages 28-30			
Q	Option	Answer	Correct Spelling
Eg	D	DRED	DREAD
1	E	LITRALLY	LITERALLY
2	B	HERITIGE	HERITAGE
3	D	FLUORECSENT	FLUORESCENT
4	B	KINDERGARDEN	KINDERGARTEN
5	A	WEEVE	WEAVE
6	C	DARSTARDLY	DASTARDLY
7	E	RUSTICK	RUSTIC
8	D	KERFUFLE	KERFUFFLE
9	B	ERATIC	ERRATIC
10	A	CONTINUM	CONTINUUM
11	C	IMPITUS	IMPETUS
12	B	SNUFLE	SNUFFLE
13	C	GRASE	GRAZE
14	A	ADOOR	ADORE
15	C	BOOL	BALL
16	E	QUARY	QUARRY
17	B	TRED	TREAD
18	D	LITRATE	LITERATE
19	C	JOVIEL	JOVIAL
20	A	VAGERY	VAGARY
21	E	YOLKE	YOLK
22	B	RECEEPT	RECEIPT
23	C	PLUC	PLUCK
24	D	MITAGATE	MITIGATE
25	E	CORAGE	COURAGE
26	A	DISMIS	DISMISS
27	B	ENGROSE	ENGROSS
28	C	UNWELDY	UNWIELDLY
29	D	ZODIAK	ZODIAC
30	E	TRADGEDY	TRAGEDY
31	A	COLOQUIAL	COLLOQUIAL
32	A	LAVAE	LARVAE
33	C	STRATIGIES	STRATEGIES
34	D	REPITITION	REPETITION
35	B	GHAUSTLY	GHASTLY
36	A	INCONVENENCE	INCONVENIENCE

Test 7 - Partial Words

For each question, fill in the missing letters to complete the word so that it matches the definition given.

Q	Answer	Q	Answer
Pages 31-34			
Eg	ABUNDANCE		
1	HUMILIATE	19	FORTUNATE
2	SILHOUETTE	20	FALLIBLE
3	EPILOGUE	21	GLIMMER
4	ACCOMPANY	22	DISSOLVE
5	MONOLOGUE	23	ERRANT
6	INSECURE	24	PUNCTURE
7	COMMEND	25	QUENCH
8	ENCOURAGE	26	CEMETERY
9	COINCIDENCE	27	HOSPITALITY
10	LUNATIC	28	ROMANCE
11	EMPATHIZE	29	PERSEVERE
12	SURPLUS	30	ARTIFICIAL
13	PROFOUND	31	COHERENT
14	REGAL	32	SUCCUMB
15	JEOPARDISE	33	PINNACLE
16	PACIFIST	34	TRAVESTY
17	FASCINATING	35	MELANCHOLY
18	COWARDLY	36	AUDIENCE

Test 8 - Synonyms and Antonyms

For each question, fill in the missing letters to complete the words so that they form synonyms and antonyms of the given word.

Q	Synonym	Antonym	Explanation
Pages 35-38			
Eg	SHY	BOLD	The words SHY and BOLD are a synonym and antonym respectively of the word COY.
1	EDUCATED	IGNORANT	The words EDUCATED and IGNORANT are a synonym and antonym respectively of the word KNOWLEDGEABLE.
2	COURAGE	COWARDICE	The words COURAGE and COWARDICE are a synonym and antonym respectively of the word BRAVERY.
3	HOSPITABLE	AUSTERE	The words HOSPITABLE and AUSTERE are a synonym and antonym respectively of the word WELCOMING.
4	COMMUNICA-TIVE	RESERVED	The words COMMUNICATIVE and RESERVED are a synonym and antonym respectively of the word FORTHCOMING.
5	BLOCKED	EMPTY	The words BLOCKED and EMPTY are a synonym and antonym respectively of the word CONGESTED.
6	MONOTONOUS	FASCINATING	The words MONOTONOUS and FASCINATING are a synonym
7	FALSEHOOD	REALITY	The words FALSEHOOD and REALITY are a synonym and anto-

Question	Synonym	Antonym	Explanation
8	DISORGANISED	EFFICIENT	The words DISORGANISED and EFFICIENT are a synonym and antonym respectively of the word FORGETFUL.
9	EXPLANATION	COMPLICATION	The words EXPLANATION and COMPLICATION are a synonym and antonym respectively of the word ILLUSTRATION.
10	PRETENTIOUS	HUMBLE	The words PRETENTIOUS and HUMBLE are a synonym and antonym respectively of the word GRANDIOSE.
11	PECULIAR	ORDINARY	The words PECULIAR and ORDINARY are a synonym and antonym respectively of the word PARTICULAR.
12	PUGNACIOUS	SYMPATHETIC	The words PUGNACIOUS and SYMPATHETIC are a synonym and antonym respectively of the word CONFRONTATIONAL.
13	ENCROACH	AVOID	The words ENCROACH and AVOID are a synonym and antonym respectively of the word IMPINGE.
14	ESSENTIAL	AUXILIARY	The words ESSENTIAL and AUXILIARY are a synonym and antonym respectively of the word NECESSARY.
15	FATE	COINCIDENCE	The words FATE and COINCIDENCE are a synonym and antonym respectively of the word DESTINY.
16	HIDEOUS	CHARMING	The words HIDEOUS and CHARMING are a synonym and antonym respectively of the word GROTESQUE.
17	IMITATION	ORIGINAL	The words IMITATION and ORIGINAL are a synonym and antonym respectively of the word FORGERY.
18	SHAME	DELIGHT	The words SHAME and DELIGHT are a synonym and antonym respectively of the word EMBARRASS.
19	LOATHSOME	HONOURABLE	The words LOATHSOME and HONOURABLE are a synonym and antonym respectively of the word DESPICABLE.
20	FLEETING	ENDURING	The words FLEETING and ENDURING are a synonym and antonym respectively of the word TRANSIENT.
21	STUBBORN	YIELDING	The words STUBBORN and YIELDING are a synonym and antonym respectively of the word OBSTINATE.
22	PALLID	GLOWING	The words PALLID and GLOWING are a synonym and antonym respectively of the word SALLOW.
23	CONFUSE	CLARIFY	The words CONFUSE and CLARIFY are a synonym and antonym respectively of the word FLUMMOX.
24	HURTFUL	CONSIDERATE	The words HURTFUL and CONSIDERATE are a synonym and antonym respectively of the word SPITEFUL.
25	CAUTIOUSNESS	ASSERTIVENESS	The words CAUTIOUSNESS and ASSERTIVENESS are a synonym and antonym respectively of the word TREPIDATION.
26	BENEFIT	MISFORTUNE	The words BENEFIT and MISFORTUNE are a synonym and antonym respectively of the word ADVANTAGE.
27	DUPLICITOUS	SINCERE	The words DUPLICITOUS and SINCERE are a synonym and antonym respectively of the word INSIDIOUS.
28	STRAY	CITIZEN	The words STRAY and CITIZEN are a synonym and antonym respectively of the word OUTCAST.

Q	Synonym	Antonym	Explanation
29	PRETEN-TIOUS	SUBDUED	The words PRETENTIOUS and SUBDUED are a synonym and antonym respectively of the word FLAMBOYANT.
30	COORDI-NATE	DISORGANISE	The words COORDINATE and DISORGANISE are a synonym and antonym respectively of the word SYNCHRONIZE.
32	CORPOREAL	SPIRITUAL	The words CORPOREAL and SPIRITUAL are a synonym and antonym respectively of the word PHYSICAL.
32	RECOGNI-TION	DISCOURTE-SY	The words RECOGNITION and DISCOURTESY are a synonym and antonym respectively of the word GRATITUDE.
33	UNGAINLY	GRACEFUL	The words UNGAINLY and GRACEFUL are a synonym and antonym respectively of the word AWKWARD.
34	INFORMAL	PEDANTIC	The words INFORMAL and PEDANTIC are a synonym and antonym respectively of the word RELAXED.
35	GORGE	EJECT	The words GORGE and EJECT are a synonym and antonym respectively of the word DEVOUR.
36	WAVER	REMAIN	The words WAVER and REMAIN are a synonym and antonym respectively of the word FLUCTUATE.

Test 9 - Sets of Synonyms

For each question, circle the letter above the set of words that are most similar in meaning to the given word. Choose one out of the four options.

Pages 39-44						
Q	Answer	Word 1	Word 2	Word 3	Word 4	Explanation
Eg	B	abruptly	violently	roughly	harshly	The words ABRUPTLY, VIOLENTLY, ROUGHLY and HARSHLY are synonyms for BRUSQUELY.
1	C	downcast	despondent	wretched	pitiful	The words DOWNCAST, DESPONDENT, WRETCHED and PITIFUL
2	A	heartless	unfeeling	ruthless	brutal	The words HEARTLESS, UNFEELING, RUTHLESS and BRUTAL are synonyms for CALLOUS.
3	B	kind	caring	gentle	amiable	The words KIND, CARING, GENTLE and AMIABLE are synonyms for BENIGN.
4	C	ambigu-ous	obscure	arguable	debatable	The words AMBIGUOUS, OBSCURE, ARGUABLE and DEBATABLE are synonyms for EQUIVOCAL.
5	D	reserved	reticent	distant	aloof	The words RESERVED, RETICENT, DISTANT and ALOOF are synonyms for TACITURN.

Q	Answer	Word 1	Word 2	Word 3	Word 4	Explanation
6	C	misconception	fantasy	dream	illusion	The words MISCONCEPTION, FANTASY, DREAM and ILLUSION are synonyms for DELUSION.
7	B	outcome	result	repercus-sion	effect	The words OUTCOME, RESULT, REPERCUSSION and EFFECT are synonyms for CONSEQUENCE.
8	D	business	company	society	club	The words BUSINESS, COMPANY, SOCIETY and CLUB are synonyms for ORGANISATION.
9	A	succinct	brief	concise	abrupt	The words SUCCINCT, BRIEF, CONCISE and ABRUPT are synonyms for TERSE.
10	B	irritate	agitate	annoy	vex	The words IRRITATE, AGITATE, ANNOY and VEX are synonyms for IRK.
11	A	glaring	obvious	overt	blatant	The words GLARING, OBVIOUS, OVERT and BLATANT are synonyms for FLAGRANT.
12	C	reduce	exhaust	consume	empty	The words REDUCE, EXHAUST, CONSUME and EMPTY are synonyms for DEPLETE.
13	A	defect	failing	error	imperfec-tion	The words DEFECT, FAILING, ERROR and IMPERFECTION are synonyms for FLAW.
14	D	gesture	sign	signal	attract	The words GESTURE, SIGN, SIGNAL and ATTRACT are synonyms for BECKON.
15	C	suffering	pain	torture	anguish	The words SUFFERING, PAIN, TORTURE and ANGUISH are synonyms for AGONY.
16	B	division	breach	rift	split	The words DIVISION, BREACH, RIFT and SPLIT are synonyms for SCHISM.
17	D	malice	venom	animosity	rancour	The words MALICE, VENOM, ANIMOSITY and RANCOUR are synonyms for SPITE.
18	A	biased	preju-diced	partisan	disposed	The words BIASED, PREJUDICED, PARTISAN and DISPOSED are synonyms for PARTIAL.
19	A	admirer	disciple	enthusiast	supporter	The words ADMIRER, DISCIPLE, ENTHUSIAST and SUPPORTER are synonyms for DEVOTEE.

Q	Answer	Word 1	Word 2	Word 3	Word 4	Explanation
20	B	wilt	decay	corrode	rot	The words WILT, DECAY, CORRODE and ROT are synonyms for WITHER.
21	C	recognised	common	ordinary	routine	The words RECOGNISED, COMMON, ORDINARY and ROUTINE are synonyms for FAMILIAR.
22	D	kingdom	territory	province	realm	The words KINGDOM, TERRITORY, PROVINCE and REALM are synonyms for EMPIRE.
23	A	explanation	rationale	pretext	vindica-tion	The words EXPLANATION, RATIONALE, PRETEXT and VINDICATION are synonyms for JUSTIFICATION.
24	B	prompt	stimulate	drive	inspire	The words PROMPT, STIMULATE, DRIVE and INSPIRE are synonyms for MOTIVATE.
25	A	involve	implicate	entangle	ensnare	The words INVOLVE, IMPLICATE, ENTANGLE and ENSNARE are synonyms for EMBROIL.
26	C	banal	ordinary	prosaic	humdrum	The words BANAL, ORDINARY, PROSAIC and HUMDRUM are synonyms for MUNDANE.
27	A	portion	share	part	percent-age	The words PORTION, SHARE, PART and PERCENTAGE are synonyms for PROPORTION.
28	D	ponder	reflect	contem-plate	consider	The words PONDER, REFLECT, CONTEMPLATE and CONSIDER are synonyms for MUSE.
29	B	unavoidable	inexorable	inescapa-ble	assured	The words UNAVOIDABLE, INEXORABLE, INESCAPABLE and ASSURED are synonyms for INEVITABLE.
30	C	exuberant	ostenta-tious	showy	animated	The words EXUBERANT, OSTENTATIOUS, SHOWY and ANIMATED are synonyms for FLAMBOYANT.

Test 10 - Mixed Test- Perfect the Grammar

For each question, circle the letter of the only option with wholly correct grammar. Choose one out of the four options.

Pages 46-47		
Q	Answer	Explanation
1	D	A comma is required after 'milk' and 'bread' to separate the items in the list.
2	D	'Who's' is a contraction of the words 'who is'. As it is a question, it needs a question mark at the end. The question mark goes inside the speech marks.
3	B	An apostrophe is required for the contraction 'wouldn't'. An apostrophe is required for the contraction 'it's'.
4	A	The correct form of the verb is 'would'. The correct form of the word is 'hanged'.
5	C	The correct form of the verb is 'bade'.
6	A	A semicolon is required to indicate that the two clauses are related.
7	D	The interrogative pronoun 'who' is required to form the question. As it is a question, it needs a question mark at the end.
8	C	The determiner 'fewer' is required as it is used with plural nouns, whereas 'less' refers to singular nouns. The word 'cups' is required because it is a plural noun.
9	A	An apostrophe is required for the contraction 'don't'. An apostrophe is required for the contraction 'aren't'.
10	C	The conjunction 'whether' is required to link the two halves of the sentence. The correct verb is 'lend'.

Test 10 - Mixed Test- Sentence Completion

For each question, circle the letter next to the word that best completes the sentence. Choose one out of the five options.

Pages 48-49			
Q	Answer	Word	Explanation
1	C	quick-tempered	Mr Banks had been particularly **quick-tempered** that day, and kicked Jack out of the class.
2	E	box	To apologise, she presented him with a **box** of chocolates.
3	D	aimlessly	I wandered **aimlessly** around town waiting for my train.
4	A	treason	Guy Fawkes attempted to kill his monarch, which is an act of **treason**.
5	E	wager	The policemen decided to make a **wager** over the racing outcome.
6	D	initiative	They had lost the map, but Zara used her **initiative** and asked a local for directions.
7	A	commiserations	Unfortunately, Kiran had not been successful, so I offered him my **commiserations**.
8	B	encouragingly	"I thought you were the best," said Maia **encouragingly**.
9	D	climax	The play's climax was the main character's betrayal.
10	E	gastronomy	He wanted to be a chef, but soon realised he didn't know the first thing about **gastronomy**.

Test 10 - Mixed Test- Change A Letter

For each question, change one letter to create a new word that matches the definition given. Write the new word in the space provided.

Page 50		
Q	Answer	Explanation
1	**F**LUSTER	Change B to F
2	**E**NSURE	Change I to E
3	DU**A**L	Change E to A
4	BRO**A**CH	Change the second O to A
5	B**E**RTH	Change I to E
6	AS**C**ENT	Change the second S to C
7	AB**J**URE	Change D to B
8	CHAF**E**	Change the second F to E
9	TUR**G**ID	Change B to G
10	**D**EBUT	Change R to D

Test 10 - Mixed Test- Left Over Word

For each question, rearrange the words in the correct order and write a sentence. Underline the extra, unnecessary word.

Page 51		
Q	Answer	Explanation
1	I	Students should have three hours' homework each night.
2	again	Careless talk costs lives.
3	bouncing	The frizbee ricocheted across the room and off the ceiling.
4	girl	The student lamented his weak grade.
5	an-tonymns	Apathy and indifference are synonyms.
6	grinning	She anticipated objections and was not disappointed.
7	learn	Shuffled sentences require concentration.
8	I'm	We have a two week holiday for Easter.
9	cake	The children are waiting in a café.
10	them	I told the babysitter I don't need sleep.

Test 10 - Mixed Test- Shuffled Sentences

For each question, rearrange the words in the correct order to form a sentence.

Page 52	
Q	Answer
1	The nurse skillfully prepared the anaesthetic.
2	They had been captured at Dunkirk.
3	I hungrily gobbled my breakfast and thoroughly brushed my teeth.
4	They accepted the tragedy and moved on.
5	She gave a nonchalant response to his questioning.
6	I have never been afraid of the dark.
7	Wrath is one of the seven deadly sins.
8	Unfortunately, your hypothesis is incorrect.
9	The farm looked unconventional and almost resembled an office block.
10	The glitch in the system meant the results were scrambled.

Test 10 - Mixed Test- Spelling Error

For each question, circle the letter above the word that is spelt incorrectly. Choose one out of the five options.

Page 53			
Q	Option	Answer	Correct Spelling
1	E	TRAMPALINE	TRAMPOLINE
2	C	YOGHUT	YOGHURT
3	B	BROOZE	BRUISE
4	E	PRESISE	PRECISE
5	A	FORFATE	FORFEIT
6	C	EXCENTRIC	ECCENTRIC
7	D	THAUGHT	THOUGHT
8	D	NOTIBLE	NOTABLE
9	B	MUSTACHE	MOUSTACHE
10	C	RICOSHETED	RICOCHETED

Test 10 - Mixed Test- Partial Words

For each question, fill in the missing letters to complete the word so that it matches the

Page 54				
Q	Answer	Question	Answer
1	CAPTIVATE	6	DELINQUENT
2	CONGESTED	7	MALIGNANT
3	TEMPORARY	8	NEUROTIC
4	CAMPAIGN	9	FATHOM
5	REMINISCE	10	BRAVADO

Test 10 - Mixed Test- Synonyms and Antonyms

For each question, fill in the missing letters to complete the words so that they form synonyms and antonyms of the given word.

	Page 55		
Q	Synonym	Antonym	Explanation
1	CONSPICUOUS	SUBTLE	The words CONSPICUOUS and SUBTLE are a synonym and antonym respectively of the word OVERT.
2	TOLERANT	FRUSTRATED	The words TOLERANT and FRUSTRATED are a synonym and antonym respectively of the word PATIENT.
3	SUPPOSE	DISBELIEVE	The words SUPPOSE and DISBELIEVE are a synonym and antonym respectively of the word PRESUME.
4	DISINTERESTED	EXCITED	The words DISINTERESTED and EXCITED are a synonym and antonym respectively of the word UNCONCERNED.
5	CATASTROPHE	TRIUMPH	The words CATASTROPHE and TRIUMPH are a synonym and antonym respectively of the word FIASCO.
6	VICAR	CONGREGA-TION	The words VICAR and CONGREGATION are a synonym and antonym respectively of the word PRIEST.
7	ABIDE	DISALLOW	The words ABIDE and DISALLOW are a synonym and antonym respectively of the word TOLERATE.
8	GOSSIP	PRAISE	The words GOSSIP and PRAISE are a synonym and antonym respectively of the word SLANDER.
9	LAWLESSNESS	AUTHORITY	The words LAWLESSNESS and AUTHORITY are a synonym and antonym respectively of the word ANARCHY.
10	PLENTIFUL	MEAGRE	The words PLENTIFUL and MEAGRE are a synonym and antonym respectively of the word BOUNTIFUL.

Test 10 - Mixed Test- Sets of Synonyms

For each question, circle the letter above the set of words that are most similar in meaning to

Pages 56-57						
Q	Option	Word 1	Word 2	Word 3	Word 4	Explanation
1	C	exuberant	ostentatious	showy	animated	The words EXUBERANT, OSTENTATIOUS, SHOWY and ANIMATED are synonyms for FLAMBOYANT.
2	B	tedious	monotonous	dreary	dull	The words TEDIOUS, MONOTONOUS, DREARY and DULL are synonyms for TIRESOME.
3	B	celebratory	jubilant	merry	jovial	The words CELEBRATORY, JUBILANT, MERRY and JOVIAL are synonyms for FESTIVE.
4	A	raucous	unruly	disorderly	boisterous	The words RAUCOUS, UNRULY, DISORDERLY and BOISTEROUS are synonyms for ROWDY.
5	D	overemotional	delirious	frenzied	frantic	The words FRANTIC, DELIRIOUS, FRENZIED and OVEREMOTIONAL are synonyms for HYSTERICAL.
6	C	diligent	thorough	painstaking	scrupulous	The words DILIGENT, THOROUGH, PAINSTAKING and SCRUPULOUS are synonyms for METICULOUS.
7	A	arrogant	proud	conceited	haughty	The words ARROGANT, PROUD, CONCEITED and HAUGHTY are synonyms for POMPOUS.
8	C	friendly	social	amiable	convivial	The words FRIENDLY, SOCIAL, AMIABLE and CONVIVIAL are synonyms for GREGARIOUS.
9	D	create	produce	conjure	foster	The words CREATE, PRODUCE, CONJURE and FOSTER are synonyms for GENERATE.
10	B	wealthy	prosperous	rich	flush	The words WEALTHY, PROSPEROUS, RICH and FLUSH are synonyms for AFFLUENT.